W9-BZC-125

Beginning BASKETBALL

Coach Jim Klinzing, Coach Mike Klinzing, and the following athletes were photographed for this book:
Rob Byrne,
Cara Cashin,
Carnel Edwards,
Tim Helms,
Chris Hull,
Beth James,
Jackie Kosmider,
Kate Kozub,
Ray Logan,
Josh Morgan,
Allison Pender,
Amy Picard,
Theresa Roach.

Beginning
BASKETBALL

Julie Jensen

Adapted from *Fundamental Basketball*
by Jim Klinzing and Mike Klinzing

Lerner Publications Company ● Minneapolis

The Beginning Sports series was conceptualized by editor Julie Jensen, designed by graphic artist Michael Tacheny, and composed on a Macintosh computer by Robert Mauzy. The Beginning Sports series was designed in conjunction with the Fundamental Sports series to offer young athletes a basic understanding of various sports at two reading levels.

Website address: www.lernerbooks.com

Photo Acknowledgments
Photographs on pp. 4–5, 6, 16 (right), 18, 19, 20, 21, 22, 24, 25, 26, 27, 30, 32, 33, 34 (right), 35, 38, 39, 40, 41, 43, 44, 46, 47, 48, 49 (middle and bottom), 50, 51 (left), 53, 54, 55, 56, 58, 59 (left), 60, 62 (left), 64, 65, 67, 72, by David Liam Kyle. Photographs on pp. 2–3, 12, 28, 29, 31, 36, 37, 49 (top), 51 (right), 61 (left), 62 (right), 63, 69, by Andy King.

Other photographs reproduced with the permission of: p. 7, University of Kansas Athletic Department; pp. 8, 9, Naismith Memorial Basketball Hall of Fame; p. 10 (bottom), 11 (left), Bettmann Archives; pp. 10 (top), 66 (top right), Robert Tringali Jr./Sports-Chrome East/West; pp. 11 (center and right), 17, 23, 59 (right), 66 (bottom), Brian Drake/SportsChrome East/West; p. 13, AP/Wide World; pp. 16 (left), 61 (right), Vincent Manniello/SportsChrome East/West; p. 34 (left), © PVA/Sports 'n Spokes, photo by Curt Beamer; p. 66 (top left), David L. Johnson/Sports-Chrome East/West.

Diagrams by Laura Westlund.

Library of Congress Cataloging-in-Publication Data

Jensen, Julie, 1957–
    Beginning basketball / Julie Jensen ; adapted from Fundamental basketball by Jim Klinzing and Mike Klinzing ; photographs by David Kyle and Andy King.
        p. cm. — (Beginning sports)
    Includes bibliographical references and index.
    Summary: Introduces the history, rules, and some famous players of basketball, as well as the fundamental skills and conditioning required for this sport.
    ISBN 0-8225-3508-4 (alk. paper)
    1. Basketball — Juvenile literature. [1. Basketball.] I. Kyle, David (David Liam), ill. II. King, Andy, ill. III. Klinzing, James E. Fundamental basketball. IV. Title. V. Series.
GV885.1.J45 1996
796.323 — dc20   96-7612

Manufactured in the United States of America
2 3 4 5 6 7 GPS 04 03 02 01 00 99

Contents

Chapter 1

HOW THIS GAME GOT STARTED

Basketball is a fun and fast game. Players hustle all over the court, trying to put the basketball through the other team's hoop. When their team has control of the ball, the players pass it to each other and shoot it at the basket. The team that doesn't have the ball scrambles to get control of it. These players guard the other team and try to steal the ball from its players. When a shot doesn't go through the hoop but bounces off the rim, players from both teams jump to grab the ball. Basketball is a game of almost nonstop action!

James Naismith invented the game of basketball while teaching in Massachusetts. He later taught at the University of Kansas, where this photograph was taken.

The Early Years

James Naismith was an instructor at the YMCA Training School in Springfield, Massachusetts. He wanted to create an indoor game that would be fun and challenging for his class during the winter. One December day in 1891, he had an idea.

Naismith got a soccer ball. He hung a peach basket at each end of the gym floor. The baskets were hung from a balcony about 10 feet off the floor. He divided his class into two teams of nine players each. He told the players to try to throw the soccer ball into the other team's basket.

The players could not **dribble**, or bounce the ball on the floor. They couldn't jump while shooting either. When the ball went out of bounds, the players dashed after it. The first team to touch the ball got it. When a player put the ball into the other team's basket, his team got one point. A custodian removed the ball from the basket after a score. The baskets made *basketball* a good name for Naismith's new game.

THE FIRST GAME

This illustration of the new game of basketball was drawn in 1892 by a student at Springfield College. The drawing was printed in the student newspaper.

Naismith, on the right in the center row, coached this group of young men in his new game—basketball. This team, which played in the winter of 1891-92, was the first basketball team.

The young men in Naismith's class quickly learned his new game. As they graduated and left the YMCA school, they spread the game across the country. The first women's game was played in Springfield in March of 1892.

Metal hoops replaced peach baskets as goals in 1893. Backboards were added in 1895, making the **bank shot** possible. By 1913, the players began to dribble to move the ball instead of always passing to each other. Several other rule changes were made in the 1930s.

The first league to pay its players was the National Basketball League, which was formed in 1898. It lasted just two years. Other professional leagues tried and failed.

Another National Basketball League (NBL) was created in 1937. The Basketball Association of America (BAA) began play in 1946.

The NBL and BAA merged in 1949 to form the National Basketball Association (NBA). A rival league, the American Basketball Association, began in 1967, but it was absorbed by the NBA in 1976.

The women's basketball team of the United States won the gold in the 1984, 1988, and 1996 Olympics.

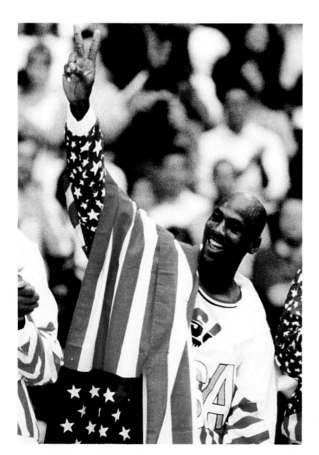

Michael Jordan and the U.S. men's basketball team won Olympic gold in 1992 and 1996.

Around the World

Basketball has been played around the world for more than 50 years. The first Olympic basketball games were played in Germany in 1936. The American men's team won every gold medal until 1972.

Players all over the world are getting better. There are now dozens of foreign-born basketball players in the NBA. One of the best known stars is Hakeem Olajuwon, who was born in Nigeria.

Boys and girls all over the world are practicing basketball. They love this game and want to be the best. You can also become a very good player!

Great Big Men

George Mikan was the first outstanding tall player in the National Basketball Association. He went to DePaul University. After college, he led the Minneapolis Lakers to four NBA titles.

The Boston Celtics were the best professional basketball team in the 1950s and '60s. Bill Russell, 6 feet and 10 inches, joined the Celtics in 1956. He led them to the NBA championship. After losing to Bob Pettit and the St. Louis Hawks the next season, the Celtics won eight championships.

During these years, Russell had many classic battles with the NBA's other outstanding big man, 7-foot-1-inch Wilt "The Stilt" Chamberlain. Chamberlain was the only player to score 100 points in a game.

While the Celtics dominated the NBA, the University of California at Los Angeles Bruins won 10 college titles in 12 years. The Bruins won their first title in 1964. After UCLA won again the next year, a 7-foot-2-inch freshman named Lew Alcindor joined the team. In Alcindor's first varsity game, he scored 56 points. He led the Bruins to three straight championships. Later Alcindor changed his name to Kareem Abdul-Jabbar. He scored more than 35,000 points in his NBA career!

Two current great big men are Hakeem Olajuwon of the Houston Rockets and Shaquille O'Neal of the Los Angeles Lakers.

Bill Russell

Kareem Abdul-Jabbar

Shaquille O'Neal

Chapter 2

BASICS

To play basketball, you need to know the basic rules and moves. You probably already know that you want to score more points than your opponent. To do this, your team must be able to score when it has the ball on offense. When your team doesn't have the ball, you and your teammates must play defense.

The Court

You can practice basketball on a playground, driveway, alley, or even in your basement. Organized games are played on a regulation court. The diagram on the next page shows a regulation high school court. The diagram also shows the markings you'll see on the court. Many courts are smaller than regulation courts. These smaller courts are fine, especially for practice.

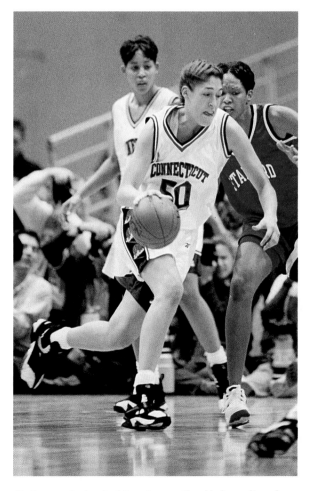

Rebecca Lobo led her team, the University of Connecticut Huskies, to an undefeated season and the NCAA women's college basketball championship in 1995.

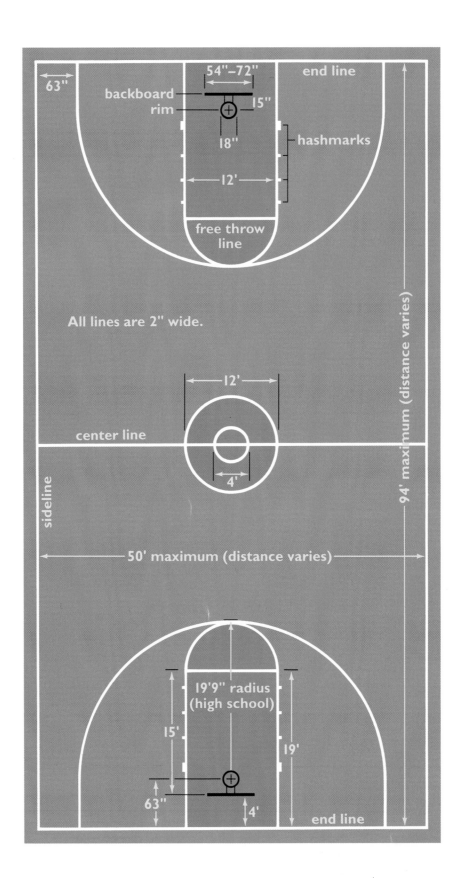

The Court

On every court, the free throw line is 15 feet from the front of the backboard. The width of the **free throw lane** is 12 feet for most games. The free throw lane is 16 feet wide on an NBA court. The free throw lane is often painted, so the lane is sometimes called "the paint."

The rim of the basket is 10 feet above the floor. But you don't have to start out with a basket that high. If your family puts a basket on the driveway, try to buy one with adjustable heights. As you grow, raise the basket. Below is a guide for the proper basket height.

Rectangular Backboard

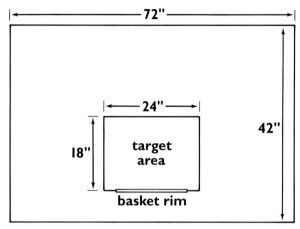

Fan-Shaped Backboard

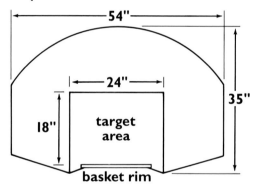

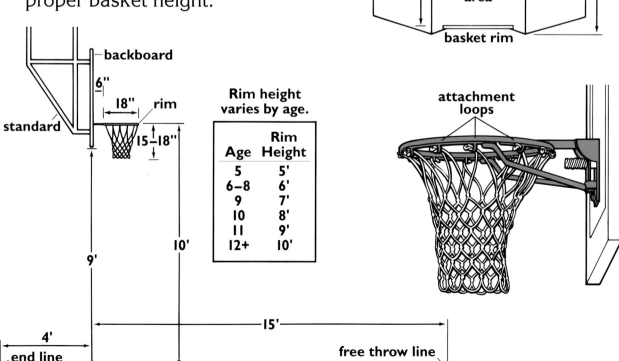

Rim height varies by age.

Age	Rim Height
5	5'
6–8	6'
9	7'
10	8'
11	9'
12+	10'

The Shot Clock

The National Basketball Association began using a shot clock in the 1954-55 season. A team has 24 seconds to take a shot. Two clocks, one above each basket, keep track of the time. The clocks start when a team takes control of the ball. If a shot bounces off the rim, the clocks are restarted at 24 seconds. If a team doesn't take a shot that scores or hits the rim within the 24 seconds, a buzzer sounds. Then the defending team gets the ball.

Youth and high school games don't use a shot clock. Women's college and international basketball games have a 30-second shot clock. In men's college basketball, the shot clock is 35 seconds.

The shot clock was added to increase the speed of the game. The shot clock forces a team to try to score quickly. Players learn to take a good shot when they can. If they wait too long, the defense may not allow another good shot.

Defenders know they won't have to chase the other team for long. The defensive players can play very hard for brief bursts.

Equipment

A men's basketball is 30 inches around. A women's basketball is 28.5 inches around.

Rubber basketballs cost less than other basketballs. They can be used outdoors and indoors. An artificial leather ball is also made for indoor and outdoor play. The best kind of ball is made of leather. Leather basketballs are expensive. They are for indoor use only.

Every basketball player needs a pair of thick-soled shoes. Running and jumping causes a lot of pounding on a player's legs and feet. Thick soles absorb these shocks. The rest of your practice uniform can be a T-shirt and shorts.

Basketballs are most often orange or brown. A basketball weighs about 20 ounces and has a pebble-grain covering.

Positions

Each team has five players on the court during a game. The center plays close to the basket. This player must **rebound** and shoot.

A team has two forwards. The power forward plays closer to the basket than the other forward. The power forward does many of the same skills as the center, but he or she is often shorter. The other forward, called a small forward, shoots from longer distances.

A team has two guards. The point guard brings the ball up the court and gets the ball to teammates, so that they can score. The fifth player is the shooting guard. This player is a good shooter and passer.

Rules

A high school basketball game is divided into four eight-minute periods, or quarters. College games have just two 20-minute halves. NBA games have four 12-minute quarters. After the first two periods or the first half, there is a 10-minute rest period called halftime.

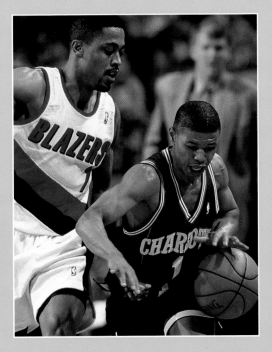

Mugsy Bogues

Never Too Little

Do you have to be tall to be a good basketball player? Tyrone "Mugsy" Bogues doesn't think so. At 5 feet 4 inches, Mugsy has always been the littlest player on his team. He practiced and worked hard to improve his skills. Mugsy became the starting guard for the Charlotte Hornets of the National Basketball Association. Why? Because he never listened to anyone saying he was too small.

Anthony "Spud" Webb is 5 feet 7 inches tall. He has played in the NBA for more than 10 years. He won the 1986 NBA Slam Dunk Championship with a fantastic display of dunking ability. Spud is also a great passer and can sink his shot. In other words, he has mastered the skills of the game.

The game begins with a jump ball at the center of the court. The referee tosses the ball up between a player from each team. Each player tries to tap the ball to a teammate.

This is the only jump ball of the game. The team that wins the opening jump ball also gets the ball at the start of the fourth quarter. The other team gets the ball at the start of the second and third quarters. When opposing players both grasp the ball and try to pull it away, a held ball is called. After a held ball, the ball is given to the teams on an alternate basis.

Violations

You must dribble with one hand at a time. If you touch the ball with both hands at the same time, you must pass or take a shot. If you start to dribble again, you will be called for a **violation.** This violation is a **double dribble.**

When you are holding the ball, one foot must stay put. That foot is called your "pivot" foot. You can't move this foot unless you are dribbling or you'll be called for **traveling.** You can rotate on your pivot foot while your other foot steps in any direction.

A team has 10 seconds to move the ball past the mid-court line. Once past the center line, a team can't let the ball go into its **backcourt** unless an opponent touched the ball last.

A three-second violation is called if a player on the team with the ball stays in the free throw lane for more than three seconds.

After a team scores, the other team throws the ball in bounds from underneath the basket. The player throwing in the ball can move anywhere behind the endline. Any other time a player throws the ball in bounds, he or she must keep one foot set or the other team gets the ball.

Technical Fouls

A referee calls a technical foul when a player or coach does or says something wrong. Some examples of what will earn a technical are: fighting, throwing the ball at another player, arguing, or swearing.

If your team is given a technical foul, a player from the other team gets to shoot two free throws. Then the other team gets the ball. Your opponent could score five points on the play.

Giving your competition five points can cost your team a victory. Keep your cool and play smart.

Fouls and Free Throws

Basketball players aren't supposed to push, pull, bump, or hit opponents. If you do these things, a **foul** should be called. The referees decide when to call a foul. Two or three referees officiate a basketball game.

When opposing players bump into one another, a referee must decide which player ran into the other. The player who moved to the spot of the collision first is said to have had "position." The player arriving to the spot second committed the foul. A block is a foul on the defensive player. A charge is a foul on the offensive player.

Players are allowed five fouls before they must leave the game. (The NBA allows players to have six fouls.)

A player who is fouled while shooting gets to shoot a **free throw.** The other players can't bother the shooter during a free throw. The other players also can't step into the lane before the ball touches the rim. If a player who isn't shooting is fouled, that player's team gets the ball out of bounds.

Bonus free throws are award-ed to a team when its opponents commit more than six fouls during a half of the game. The bonus means that even if a player wasn't shooting when he or she was fouled, that player gets to shoot a free throw. If the player makes the free throw, he or she shoots another one.

Scoring

Free throws are worth one point. Any shot other than a free throw is called a **field goal.** A field goal scores two points. If the shooter makes a shot from beyond the three-point line, that shot is worth three points.

Chapter 3

SKILLS

The main goal of basketball is to score more points than your opponent. You must be able to dribble, pass, rebound, and play defense. Still, putting the ball into the basket is the most important skill in this game.

Shooting

Most players love to practice shooting. There are three types of shots every player needs: a **set shot**, a **jump shot**, and a **layup.**

When you practice shooting, remember the letters **B-E-E-F + C.** Each letter stands for an element of good shooting form.

Hakeem Olajuwon was a big reason the Houston Rockets won back-to-back NBA championships in 1994 and 1995.

23

The **B** stands for *balance*. Allison's feet are slightly wider than shoulder width apart. Her knees are bent so that she can spring off the floor. Her weight is balanced.

The first **E** stands for *elbow in*. Allison brings the ball to chest level on her shooting-hand side. Her elbow is directly under the ball. Allison keeps her elbow close to her body so that her shot is in line with the basket.

The second **E** stands for *eyes on target*. Allison looks at the front of the rim when she shoots. She wants to push the ball just over that spot on the rim and into the basket.

The **F** stands for *follow through*. As the ball leaves Allison's hand, her elbow straightens. The ball rolls off her fingertips. The ball never touches the palm of her shooting hand. After Allison releases the ball, she snaps her wrist.

The **C** stands for *concentration*. This is the most important part of shooting. Allison does not think about the defenders, the score, the crowd, or the referees. All she thinks about is the ball going into the basket.

● *Set Shot*

Most players use a set shot when shooting free throws. Allison is practicing her free throw shooting by working on her set shot. She places her shooting hand on the back of the ball. Her other hand is on the side of the ball. As Allison releases the ball, she rises up on her toes.

Allison has a routine she uses before every free throw. Her routine relaxes her and it helps her concentrate. She bounces the ball a couple of times. Then she takes a deep breath before shooting.

● *Jump Shot*

The jump shot is the shot play-ers use most. A jump shot is a lot like a set shot. There is one difference between a jump shot and a set shot. During a jump shot, the shooter's feet leave the floor. During a set shot, the shooter's feet stay on the floor.

Beth releases the ball at the top of her jump, before she starts coming down. This puts all her power into the shot. Beth releases the ball from above her head. She doesn't have to jump as high as she can. She jumps just high enough to shoot over her defender.

● *Layup*

To shoot a layup, Carnel dribbles toward the basket and jumps off his left foot. His right knee comes up as if it were attached by a string to his right elbow. Carnel's right hand is behind the ball. His left hand is on the side of the ball, to guide his shot. He aims for the corner of the square on the backboard. Layups can also be taken from the left side. The moves are the exact opposite.

Shoot when you are open and you have the best chance to score. Otherwise, pass the ball to a teammate.

Passing

The quickest way to move the ball up the floor is by passing. If you don't believe this, try this race. Pass a ball to someone at midcourt while a friend dribbles a ball that far. Which ball gets to the center line first?

A good pass is one that can be caught. Don't throw a hard pass when a softer pass will work. If a teammate has the ball, be ready to catch a pass. Have your hands open and your eyes on the ball.

● Chest Pass

Kate is throwing a **chest pass.** She uses both hands. Her hands are on either side of the ball. Her thumbs point toward each another. She releases the ball at chest height. As she lets go of the ball, she steps toward the receiver. She snaps her wrists and finishes with her thumbs pointing down.

● *Bounce Pass*

Ray is using a **bounce pass.** He has both hands on the ball. He aims for a spot on the floor about two-thirds of the way to his teammate. He steps toward his teammate as he releases the ball. After Ray releases the ball, he follows through with his thumbs down. The ball should bounce once on the floor. Ray's teammate should be able to catch the ball at waist level.

● Push Pass

Chris is doing a **push pass.** A push pass can bounce or not bounce. Chris uses just one hand to push the ball. His other hand is on the side of the ball to guide it. Chris snaps his wrist as he follows through.

● *Overhead Pass*

To throw an **overhead pass,** Tim grips the ball with both hands. He takes the ball above his head and brings his arms forward. Then he snaps both wrists while stepping toward his teammate. Tim aims his throw at the receiver's chin so that his teammate doesn't have to lunge to catch the ball.

Basketball on Wheels

Playing in wheelchairs allows players with lower limb disabilities to test their talent against others with similar disabilities.

Wheelchair basketball players are allowed two pushes of the chair between dribbles. A player who can move the wheelchair and still control the ball is a player to watch! Most regular basketball rules apply, including those for fouls, free throws, and out-of-bounds plays.

Many NBA teams sponsor wheelchair teams. These teams play other wheelchair teams and participate in tournaments. They also take on teams of able-bodied players who play in wheelchairs.

How about basketball on in-line skates? Yes, it is being played! If you've mastered in-line skating, give it a try. Be careful—the slam dunk may be a real adventure in this game!

Dribbling

Dribbling should be your last choice when you get the ball. See if you can shoot or pass before you think about dribbling.

● *Speed Dribble*

Beth moves the ball quickly with a **speed dribble.** She pushes the ball out in front of her body with the ends of her fingers as she runs. She doesn't look at the ball while she's dribbling.

● *Control Dribble*

When closely guarded, Beth uses a **control dribble.** She keeps her body between the ball and her defender. She keeps her head up and watches for an open teammate.

Rebounding

Grabbing the ball after a shot is missed is an exciting part of basketball. To be a good rebounder, expect that every shot will be missed. Then get into position to grab that rebound.

● *Defensive Rebounding*

When the other team is shooting, you will be trying to get a defensive rebound. Learn how to **box out** your opponents. Carnel is boxing out Ray. Carnel faces the basket. He keeps his body

between Ray and the basket. Carnel's feet are spread wide, with his arms out and his hands up. After the shot, Carnel leaps high to get the ball after it bounces off the rim.

● *Offensive Rebounding*

When your team is shooting, you will be trying to get an offensive rebound. Your opponents, meanwhile, will be trying to box out you and your teammates.

To get around the player boxing out, quickly step to the left or right. You can also fake as though you were going to move in one direction. Then, go the other way. Always hustle!

Defense

Playing defense isn't as showy as scoring points. But without a good defense, a team doesn't have the chance to score.

Jackie is in the basic defensive stance below. Her feet are spread more than shoulder width apart. Her knees are bent as if she were about to sit down but her back is straight. Her head is up so she can watch her opponent and her hands are out to each side to deflect passes.

When her opponent has the ball, Allison watches that player's belly button area. A player can fake with her head or arms, but a person's belly button goes where the player goes.

As her opponent dribbles, Allison moves sideways. She slides and keeps her body between her opponent and the basket. Allison doesn't run or cross her feet because she might trip.

If her opponent changes directions, Allison steps back with the foot nearest to where her opponent is going. She continues her defensive slide.

When you are guarding a player without the ball, your stance is the same. Raise your hands slightly to cut off passes.

If the player you are guarding doesn't have the ball, you don't need to follow him or her all over the court. If your player is on the side of the court opposite where the ball is, stay near the middle of the court. From the middle, you can help teammates if they get beat.

3–2 Zone Defense

2–3 Zone Defense

● Player-to-Player and Zone Defenses

Teams use either a **player-to-player defense** or a **zone defense.** In a player-to-player defense, each player guards another player on the opposing team. In a zone defense, each player protects an area of the court. When the ball enters your area, you guard the opposing player who has the ball. Zone defenses aren't allowed in pro basketball.

A team uses a player-to-player defense when it has five good defensive players. This defense is hard work, but it is the most effective way to prevent the other team from scoring.

A zone is a good defense when the opposing team has one outstanding strength, such as great outside shooting or a good tall center.

Zone defenses are labeled with numbers. The numbers stand for the way the defensive players are arranged, starting at midcourt and moving toward the basket being defended. Against a good outside shooting team, a coach might use a 3-2 zone. That zone defense puts three defenders out, away from the basket. A 2-3 zone puts two defenders outside and three near the basket. This defense is used against teams with good inside scorers.

Whether playing player-to-player defense or zone defense, all five defenders must work together. Next time you play basketball, try to improve your defensive skills. Coaches will like your effort, and you will love stopping your opponent.

Chapter 4

PLAY AND PRACTICE

Eric leaps high to grab the defensive rebound. He makes a chest pass to Mike, who speed dribbles upcourt.

Mike reaches the free throw line. He looks left, but bounce passes right to Ernest. Ernest goes up for a layup. The ball rolls across the rim, but it does not drop. Shawn, trailing the fast break, leaps high and lays the ball in the basket. Wow! What a play by Shawn! And he's fouled!

Shawn goes to the line for one free throw. He bounces the ball twice, eyes the basket, and smoothly strokes in the shot to complete the three-point play. The Mustangs drop back on defense. Ernest's man takes a jumper from 10 feet. The ball bounces off the rim. Shawn jumps and snares the ball. The Mustangs will be tough to beat tonight!

Joining a Youth League

Joining a youth basketball league is a great way to have fun and meet new friends. To find a league, contact the local recreation department, the high school athletic department, or look for notices in the newspaper.

Youth league coaches should teach the fundamentals to all players with plenty of fun activities. Avoid coaches who only want to win, yell at their players, or don't provide each player the chance to play and practice. Get in a league with players at your level and then get better!

Polish *your* skills by playing in pickup games on the driveway, at the park, or at school. Play as often as possible.

Try to play against players who play better than you do so you will improve. When you are playing against less talented players, work on your weak spots. For example, dribble with your left hand only, or work on your passing.

You can practice basketball skills alone. Of course, it's more fun to practice with friends. But if your friends don't want to practice as hard as you do, don't let them stop you.

If you are on a school team, your coach will plan practices during the season. During the off-season, you will be responsible for your practice. First, find a place to practice. It may be the driveway, playground, or recreation center. It may even be your basement. Here are some drills you can practice.

● Ballhandling Drills

Do each of these drills for about a minute. Even if these drills are hard at first, stick with them. Soon you will be handling the ball like a pro.

● **Body circles:** In the top photo at right, Josh and Jackie circle the ball around their bodies. They start at waist level. They circle the ball up around their heads. Then they move down to their ankles, doing one leg at a time.

● **Figure 8s:** Chris and Amy, middle photo at right, stand with their feet spread slightly wider than shoulder width apart. They move the ball in a figure-8 pattern between their legs. Then they do the drill again, moving the ball in the other direction.

● **Tipping:** Tipping the ball from hand to hand is one of Kate's favorite drills, bottom photo at right. She moves the ball from her ankles to over her head.

• **Figure 8 high-dribble and carry:** In this drill, Chris stands upright. His feet are spread slightly wider than shoulder width apart.

He dribbles the ball once backward through his legs and catches it in his other hand behind him. Chris then swings his hand and the ball forward around his waist. He dribbles once backward between his legs and catches the ball with the first hand.

● *Dribbling*

Practice dribbling with your right and left hands, and keep your head up.

• **Dribble in place:** Dribble with one hand. Then dribble with your other hand. Then dribble with your eyes closed.

• **Speed dribble and layups:** Dribble the length of the court. When you get to the free throw line, cut to the basket and shoot a layup.

• **Dribble in a zigzag pattern up and down the court:** Use your change-of-direction dribble to move downcourt.

• **Dribble up and down the court:** Cara, in the photo below, uses a speed dribble to go from baseline to baseline.

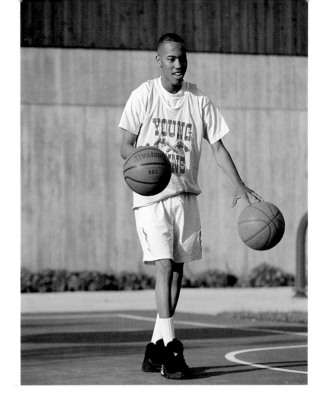

• **Double dribbles:** Dribble two balls at once, like Carnel, above.

• **Change-of-pace:** Josh varies his speed and direction while dribbling, in the photo above.

Shooting

Everyone loves to shoot! Reward yourself with shooting practice after you've worked on your other skills. Practice layups, set shots, free throws, and jump shots.

Think about B-E-E-F + C so that you remember to use correct shooting form. Keep your balance, elbow in under the ball, eyes on the rim, follow through, and concentrate only on the ball going through the basket.

• **Layups:** Allison, at left, does at least 20 layups with each hand. She practices layups from both sides of the basket.

• **Free throws:** Make a minimum of 50 free throws at every practice. Create a routine you can use for every free throw.

• **Three-point shots:** Can you use good shooting form from beyond the three-point line? Then shoot 25 three-pointers in practice. If not, wait until you are stronger to work on your three-point shot.

• **Set shots:** Tim, above, takes 10 shots from about three feet from the basket. Then he moves to another spot. He takes 50 shots from five spots.

• **Jump shots:** Ray starts close to the side of the basket. He uses the backboard and takes 10 shots. Then he moves around the court, taking at least 50 jump shots.

Practice Schedule

Practice at least three times a week for about one hour. Also, whenever you have a chance to play, do it. Here's one good practice session:

Skill	Minutes
Ballhandling	5
Shooting	15
Passing	5
Rebounding	5
Shooting	5
Defense	5
Shooting	15
Ballhandling	5

Tips:

- *Do a variety of drills for each skill.*
- *Try to get better each day.*
- *Practice with others when you can.*
- *Practice with better players.*
- *Stay positive, even when practice doesn't go so well.*

Your school work will always be your first priority. Still, you can probably find an hour a day for basketball practice.

Conditioning

In a game between players of equal skills, the players who are in better shape will usually win. You can be the best-conditioned player on the court.

Basketball players need strength to jump high for rebounds. They need endurance to hustle the entire game. Players need speed, quickness, and agility to score and to play tough defense. Develop your fitness for basketball by conditioning three days each week.

● *Jumping*

The higher you jump, the better your shooting and rebounding will be. There are several ways to improve your jumping.

Start with rope skipping. Do 100 jumps in any style. In fact, try to learn as many ways to jump rope as possible. The variety will develop your coordination. Challenge yourself.

Next, jump on a soft surface

like grass or gym mats. (Don't jump on concrete or asphalt. Hard surfaces can hurt your legs.) These drills will get you jumping higher and farther.

• Take a quick step forward and jump as high as you can. Then do this drill on the other foot. Do 10 jumps with each leg.

• Rapidly jump back and forth across a line. Jump forward, backward, and from side to side. Jump with both feet at first, then use one foot at a time. Do 10 jumps.

• Jump and throw your arms up into the air. As soon as you land, jump again. Do this 10 times.

• Skip. Swing your arms as hard as you can to get as much height as possible on each skip. Skip 20 times.

As you improve, do more of these exercises, or others that your coach suggests. Rest about one minute between each exercise. With rest, you can do your best on every drill.

● *Running*

After you jump, run. You will run your best when you use good form. Keep your head level and steady. Swing your arms forward and backward without twisting your shoulders or waist.

Stay upright but lean forward slightly. Lift your knees high when you sprint. Point your toes straight ahead and land on the balls of your feet.

Start by running for about 12 minutes. Run one or two minutes longer each practice. After six weeks, you should be running for 24 minutes. It's okay if you must walk a little at first. Learn the pace you are able to run nonstop. If you are very tired by these runs, slow down.

Once you can run nonstop for 24 minutes, work on your speed by running short sprints. Do 6 to 12 sprints on a soft surface, like grass, in each workout. These sprints should be about 20 yards long. Walk slowly back to the start after each sprint. The rest is important. It allows you to sprint at top speed. As you improve, do longer sprints.

Practice for at least one hour three days a week. Lift weights, jump, or run on the other days of the week. If you do this, your play on the basketball court will improve. Don't wait—get started!

Chapter 5

RAZZLE DAZZLE

As you improve, others will see how much better you have become in all aspects of the game. They may not know how hard you have worked in practice and on your conditioning. That's okay! You know the secret of success.

You may now be ready to add some new moves to your game. Here are some skills to practice. These moves will help you take your game to new heights.

Shots

To be a real scoring threat, you need a variety of shots. Add your own flair, and defenders will have to struggle to keep you from scoring.

Picking a Camp

Summer basketball camps are a good way to learn more about playing the game. There are two types of camps: overnight and day.

Overnight camps are most often held at colleges. Campers sleep in the dormitories and eat in the cafeteria.

Day camps are held at colleges or local high schools. Some day camps also offer half-day camps. These camps will run three or four hours a day for the week. Full-day camps provide plenty of high-level instruction and competition.

Try to attend a camp with players who are as good or better than you are. This will challenge you to work hard and improve your game.

Talk to someone who has attended the camp you are considering. Chances are, if they had a good time and improved their skills, you will too. Remember, it takes more than one week of camp to become a great player. Take home what you learn and practice.

58

● Underhand Layup

For an **underhand layup,** or finger-roll layup, the shooter softly lays the ball to the back-board with an underhand flick of the wrist.

● Hook Shots

Use the **hook shot** and the **jump hook shot** near the bas-ket. Release the ball with one hand from the side of your body, above your head.

When doing the hook shot, shown above, jump off the foot closest to the basket. To shoot a jump hook, shown on the next page, jump off both feet.

The hook shot used by Kareem Abdul-Jabbar is nicknamed the "skyhook." Abdul-Jabbar's shot seemed to come out of the sky, because he is 7 feet 2 inches tall.

● *Three-Point Shot*

Once you have proper shooting form and can keep that form while shooting from beyond the three-point line, practice three-point shots. At first, shoot a set shot as you jump toward the basket. As you get better, your jump will be more upward than forward. The three-pointer often works best after the ball has been passed inside and back out.

● *Dunk*

An adjustable-height basket is handy if you want to learn to **dunk.** The basic moves are the same as for a layup. When you get above the rim, throw the ball forcefully down with one or two hands. Add some flair by shifting the ball or your body while in the air.

Shaquille O'Neal's thundering dunks have made him a favorite with fans throughout the country and around the world.

Offensive Moves

You want to be able to get away from your defender so you can take open shots. These moves will dazzle opponents.

● Triple-Threat Position

Rob is in the triple-threat position. His knees are flexed and his head is up. Rob holds the ball with both hands at waist level. He's ready to dribble, pass, or shoot—a triple threat! Rob can also fake these moves.

● Crossover Dribble

A crossover dribble that is done well crosses up opponents. When you perform this move correctly, you won't have to worry about your defender for a while. In the photo above and in those on the next page, Ray shows how he does this move.

Ray starts by dribbling to his right. Then he plants his right foot. He quickly makes a low dribble to his left hand while he shifts direction to the left. Ray can also do this move in the opposite direction.

Ray starts his dribble going to his right, then shifts his weight and switches the ball to his left hand. His defender, Carnel, can't switch directions fast enough to stay with Ray.

● *Screens*

Setting a **screen** helps a teammate get open for an easy shot. Allison is setting a screen in the photo below. She puts herself in the path of a defender. This allows Allison's teammate, Cara, to break free from the player guarding her.

● *Baseball Pass*

The baseball pass is really thrown more like a football pass. It is a long pass that is often used for a **fast break.** Tim puts the ball behind one ear with both hands. He fires a long pass by extending his passing arm forward. Accuracy is the most important part of throwing the baseball pass. The best pass is a completed one.

Magic Johnson

Who was the Greatest?

Earvin "Magic" Johnson, Larry Bird, and Michael Jordan ignited NBA thrills during the 1980s and early '90s. Each was a college all-American. As good as they were in college, each really blossomed in the pros. Which one was the greatest player? Fans will argue a long time to try to answer that question.

Magic is 6 feet 9 inches. He played point guard as no one had before. He was a great passer and dribbler for his Los Angeles Laker teammates. He returned in 1996 after being away from the game for four and a half seasons.

Bird, at 6 feet 9 inches, was a dominating forward. Passing and shooting were his best skills. Boston Celtics fans were happy to see Larry with the ball in his hands as the game clock wound down.

Jordan could do it all at 6 feet 6 inches. No one has ever displayed such individual creativity in moves to the basket. He won seven straight scoring titles! Michael retired in 1993 after the Chicago Bulls won their third NBA title. He returned in 1995 and led the Bulls to three more titles.

Who was the best? What's your opinion?

Michael Jordan

Larry Bird

● *Fast break*

A fast break is one way to move the ball quickly up the court by passing and dribbling. The fast break usually starts after a rebound. The players on the fast break quickly spread out across the floor. If the passes are good, a fast break often ends in an easy layup.

Do you dream of being a great basketball player? The skills and ideas in this book will give you a solid base for your basketball career. No one can take away your goal. Live it, believe in it, and, most importantly, practice for it. You will love what happens.

BASKETBALL TALK

backcourt: The half of the court that has the basket a team is defending.

bank shot: A shot that is intended to gently hit the backboard and fall through the basket.

bounce pass: A pass that bounces between the passer and the receiver.

box out: A move to establish a position close to the basket while rebounding; a player faces the basket and spreads his or her feet to block the path of an opponent to the basket.

chest pass: A pass that is thrown with two hands, starting at chest height.

control dribble: A method of moving the ball with a low bounce while the player protects the ball by keeping his or her body between the opponent and the ball.

double dribble: A violation in which the player with the ball dribbles with both hands at the same time. Double dribble is also called if a player dribbles, holds the ball, and then starts dribbling again.

dribble: A continuous bouncing of the ball on the floor, using one hand.

dunk: To slam the ball through the basket from above the rim.

fast break: A quick movement of the ball downcourt by passing or dribbling in an attempt to score before the opposing team can set up its defense.

field goal: A shot that is scored while the ball is in play. A field goal is worth two points unless it is taken from beyond the three-point arc, in which case it is worth three points.

foul: An illegal act that involves physical contact with an opponent.

free throw: A chance to shoot at the basket without interference from an opponent. A free throw is awarded because of a foul by an opponent. The shot is taken from the free throw line and is worth one point.

free throw lane: A 12- or 16-foot wide portion of the court underneath each basket, between the end line of the court and the free throw line. Because these areas are often painted a different color than the rest of the court, these areas are often referred to as "the paint."

hook shot: A shot in which the shooter begins with his or her back to the basket, then pivots and sweeps the ball up and over his or her head with one hand.

jump hook shot: A hook shot during which the shooter jumps before releasing the ball.

jump shot: A shot in which the shooter jumps and releases the ball at the peak of his or her jump.

layup: A shot in which the shooter dribbles toward the basket, jumps, and gently bounces the ball off the backboard and into the basket.

Ray practices his dunk.

push pass: A pass that is thrown with one hand pushing the ball and the other hand guiding it.

rebound: To gain possession of the ball after a missed shot. An offensive rebound is a rebound by the shooting team. A defensive rebound is a rebound by the defending team.

screen: A move by an offensive player to legally block a defender's path so that the offensive player's teammate can get free for a shot or pass.

set shot: A shot that is released while both of the shooter's feet remain on the court.

speed dribble: A method of moving the ball with a high bounce while running quickly.

traveling: A violation in which the player with the ball moves both feet without bouncing the ball.

underhand layup: A layup in which the shooter's hand is palm up when the ball is released, so that the ball gently rolls off the fingers and into the basket. Also called a fingerroll layup.

violation: An illegal act that doesn't involve contact with another player.

zone defense: A style of defensive play in which each player is assigned a specific area, or zone, of the court to defend.

overhead pass: A two-handed pass that starts above the passer's head.

player-to-player defense: A style of defensive play in which each player is assigned to guard a specific player on the other team.

FURTHER READING

Anderson, Dave. *The Story of Basketball.* New York: William Morrow and Company, Inc., 1988.

Bird, Larry with John Bischoff. *Bird on Basketball.* Reading, Mass.: Addison-Wesley Publishing Company, Inc., 1985.

Gutman, Bill. *The Pictorial History of Basketball.* New York: Gallery Books, 1988.

Jacobs, A.G. *Basketball Rules in Pictures.* New York: The Putnam Publishing Group, 1989.

Klinzing, Jim and Mike Klinzing. *Basketball for Starters and Stars.* Benton, Wis.: Syskos Basketball Books and Videos, 1995.

Pruitt, Jim. *Play Better Basketball.* Chicago: Contemporary Books, Inc., 1982.

Scott, John W. *Step-By-Step Basketball Fundamentals for the Player and Coach.* Englewood Cliffs, N.J.: Prentice Hall, 1985.

Vancil, Mark. *NBA Basketball Basics.* New York: Sterling Publishing Company, Inc., 1995.

FOR MORE INFORMATION

Amateur Athletic Union of the United States
Walt Disney World Resorts
P.O. Box 10,000
Lake Buena Vista, FL 32830-1000
www.aausports.org

Basketball Congress International
1210 E. Indian School Road
Phoenix, AZ 85014

National Basketball Association
645 Fifth Avenue
New York, NY 10022
www.nba.com

National Collegiate Athletic Association
6201 College Blvd.
Overland Park, KS 66211-2422
www.ncaa.org

National Wheelchair Basketball Association
110 Seaton Building
University of Kentucky
Lexington, KY 40506
www.nwba.org

USA Basketball
5465 Mark Dabling Blvd.
Colorado Springs, CO 80918-3842
www.usabasketball.org

Youth Basketball of America, Inc.
P.O. Box 3067
Orlando, FL 32821

INDEX